PROJECT LEARNING USING DIGITAL PORTFOLIOS™

HOW TO CREATE DIGITAL PORTFOLIOS TO SHOWCASE YOUR ACHIEVEMENTS AND INTERESTS

ANITA LOUISE MCCORMICK

Rosen YA™
New York

Published in 2018 by The Rosen Publishing Group, Inc.
29 East 21st Street, New York, NY 10010

Copyright © 2018 by The Rosen Publishing Group, Inc.

First Edition

All rights reserved. No part of this book may be reproduced in any form without permission in writing from the publisher, except by a reviewer.

Library of Congress Cataloging-in-Publication Data

Names: McCormick, Anita Louise, author.
Title: How to create digital portfolios to showcase your achievements and interests / Anita Louise McCormick.
Description: New York, NY : Rosen Publishing, 2018. | Series: Project learning using digital portfolios | Includes bibliographical references and index. | Audience: Grades 7–12.
Identifiers: ISBN 9781508175346 (library bound book)
Subjects: LCSH: Electronic portfolios in education—Juvenile literature. | Digital media—Juvenile literature.
Classification: LCC LB1029.P67 M33 2018 | DDC 371.39—dc23

Manufactured in China

CONTENTS

INTRODUCTION   4

CHAPTER ONE
WHAT ARE DIGITAL PORTFOLIOS?   7

CHAPTER TWO
WHY CREATE A DIGITAL PORTFOLIO?   16

CHAPTER THREE
SKILLS FOR CREATING AN OUTSTANDING DIGITAL PORTFOLIO   27

CHAPTER FOUR
WHAT TO INCLUDE IN YOUR DIGITAL PORTFOLIO   36

CHAPTER FIVE
WHAT DIGITAL PLATFORM SHOULD I USE?   44

CHAPTER SIX
BEYOND CREATING A DIGITAL PORTFOLIO   49

GLOSSARY   55

FOR MORE INFORMATION   57

FOR FURTHER READING   59

BIBLIOGRAPHY   60

INDEX   62

INTRODUCTION

What do you think of when you hear the term "digital portfolio?" Does it make you think about something artists or photographers might create to showcase their work? Or perhaps something authors might use to present their best writing samples to a publisher?

Digital portfolios are all that and more. Whether you are a middle or high school student, attending college, a person looking for a way to effectively present their skills to potential employers, or a freelance web designer wanting to attract new clients, digital portfolios are a great way to show the world what you're capable of doing.

Creating a digital portfolio that showcases your interests and achievements can give you the platform you need to explain your interests and achievements to friends and family members. No matter where they live, by emailing a link to your digital portfolio, you can share the story of your achievements with anyone. They can read about your interests and goals and you can show them photos and videos of your latest project.

Having a digital portfolio will make it easier to present yourself to anyone, including to college admissions officers and potential employers. Applicants who have digital portfolios that show what they have already accomplished can help employers decide if they have the necessary skills to succeed at a job they're interviewing for.

Having a digital portfolio can also help you make a great impression on any group you might want to join or volunteer for. For example, if you want to volunteer to help a local animal shelter and you have years

Creating a digital portfolio that showcases your interests and achievements has many benefits.

of experience helping your family with a local dog show in your community, creating a digital portfolio about your interest in and work with dogs would help the administrator at the animal shelter understand what you're good at.

If you think you might like to start your own business someday, it will be a big help to have samples of your best work available in digital form so you can present your skills to prospective customers. In today's world, most businesses, no matter how large or small, have some kind of website or digital platform. The digital portfolio you're building now can be the beginning of the business website you build in the future.

Another advantage of having a digital portfolio is that it can help you see how your interests and achievements connect and how one interest can spark another. The story of how your interests developed and grew through the years can make interesting reading, as well as help you decide on which college or trade school you might want to attend.

While some web hosting services are costly, there are many digital platforms available that you can use to post your digital portfolio for free. All you need is a computer, an internet connection, and your ideas about the kind of digital portfolio you want to create. Most are simple to use and do not require a knowledge of coding.

This book will tell you how digital portfolios came into use, why they are so important, what you'll need to create one, and discuss some of the skills, such as video and photo editing, that will help you create a digital portfolio that presents your interests and accomplishments at their very best.

CHAPTER ONE

WHAT ARE DIGITAL PORTFOLIOS?

Nearly everyone knows that portfolios that showcase a person's best work are a tool of the trade for creative professionals. And they have been for a very long time. But their usefulness is not limited to people in artistic fields. In recent years, portfolios have become a way for people in many walks of life to collect the best samples of their work and have it available for the public to view. No matter what field you are in, having a digital portfolio can be a great way to show the world who you are and what you can do!

Most students start keeping a portfolio of some sort that showcases their work when they are in grade school. In many schools, at the beginning of a new school year, teachers give you a cardboard or plastic folder or help you set up an online digital portfolio, as a place to keep your writing assignments, drawings, and other school projects. As you add to this collection of work throughout the school year, it helps you, as well as your teachers and parents, see how much you've learned and accomplished. It also shows how your interests have developed and gives a good indication of the direction your interests and education might take in the future.

In addition to that, having samples of your best work stored online can come in handy if you need to locate a photograph, writing assignment, video recording, or other sample of your work in a hurry.

Before the digital age, nearly all portfolios were folders made of heavy paper, cardboard, or plastic. The art, photography, or writing samples inside the portfolio were also printed or drawn on paper, meaning the portfolio could only be viewed in person. Artists, for example, had to personally show or mail their portfolios to people they wanted to view their work to in hopes of getting assignments or having their work selected for display in galleries. This could make the task of having your work viewed by the right people a very time consuming process. The fact that people had to use paper

WHAT ARE DIGITAL PORTFOLIOS? | 9

For many years, artists and other creative people have used portfolios to display their work.

as a means of printing and displaying their work meant that the viewership was limited by the number of actual portfolios they were able to compile, as well as the number of places they could deliver them.

PORTFOLIOS IN THE DIGITAL AGE

But today, things have changed dramatically. While some paper portfolios are still in use, the digital world of computers, scanners, digital cameras, blog sites, and the worldwide connective technology of the internet now make it possible to create digital copies of your work and send it to digital platforms, where it can be displayed as a blog, website, or digital portfolio.

This all started in the mid-1990s, when the technology of the World Wide Web made the internet accessible to the general public. Before then, the internet was used mostly by scientists and engineers who needed a rapid means of computerized communication to share ideas. As the internet developed and more people were able to access it as a means of communication and storing and retrieving information, businesses, organizations, and individuals wanted to set up websites as a way of having an online presence where they could communicate and connect with the ever-growing digital world.

In the early years, most businesses, organizations, and individuals who wanted a website had to pay someone with computer programming knowledge to create it. Usually, this was done through the use of a coding system called HTML, or hypertext markup language. The HTML coding of a website's content instructed computers on how text, photos, and other elements should appear on computer screens. It instructed computers on what size and kind of font to use, the color of the page background, and the placement of photos, videos, or other visual elements.

THE DIGITAL REVOLUTION OPENS NEW WORLDS OF INFORMATION

As internet service became more affordable and more people gained access to the rapidly growing digital world, an increasingly large number of people wanted to do more than send email, read other people's articles, and view their images and videos. They wanted to start creating and posting content of their own! This demand for self-expression gave rise to a new kind of website business where individuals, organizations, and businesses could, with a minimum of computer knowledge, construct a simple website of their own.

As this need for having one's own place on the internet grew, more user-friendly digital platform companies such as Blogger, Blogspot, Wordpress, Wix, and Weebly started offering their services to the public. These digital platforms made it possible to create websites, blogs, and digital portfolios without any knowledge of coding. Instead, they worked with ready-made templates that allow users to fill in headlines, write articles and blogs, upload image and video files, as well as add links to other websites where viewers could see their work. Because of these technological advances, anyone who had access to the internet and wanted to have a website or digital portfolio to showcase his or her work could create one.

WEBSITE, BLOG OR DIGITAL PORTFOLIO?

While not all websites or blogs you see on the internet are digital portfolios, nearly any digital platform can be used as a digital portfolio. If you are planning to feature mostly writing samples in your digital portfolio, along with some links and photos, most blogging sites should be sufficient for your needs.

Photography- and art-centered internet platforms, such as Flickr, Behance, and Deviantart, can be used as digital portfolios, especially if the interests and achievements you want to showcase are art or photography. It all depends on the type of content you want to upload.

Digital portfolios are a great way to show off your talent as a photographer.

WHAT ARE DIGITAL PORTFOLIOS? | 13

Once you select a digital platform and create a portfolio that showcases your achievements and interests, your work becomes available to anyone connected to the digital world. You can email a link to the portfolio to anyone you want to see your work. In addition to that, anyone in the world who has a computer and connection to the internet, or even a smartphone, might find your digital portfolio in a Google search and view it!

WHO NEEDS A DIGITAL PORTFOLIO?

Basically, everyone! Many people think of artists as having portfolios, but scientists, engineers, public officials, entertainers, and people in many other professions use digital portfolios as well. In today's world, it is almost expected that people in many professions maintain a website that can include articles, blogs, photographs, videos, or sound recordings that represent the best of their work. These websites where interests, skills, and accomplishments are featured are basically digital portfolios. Search engines such as Google make it possible to look up anyone's website or digital portfolio within seconds and find out more about their work.

For example, if you are looking for a photographer to take professional photos of a special event you're planning, or maybe you need a photographer to take photos of a music group you play in, you would want to check out digital portfolios of local photographers. These portfolios

DIGITAL PORTFOLIOS SHOW YOUR SKILLS TO THE WORLD

Building a digital portfolio can be one route to starting an online business of your own.

Online businesses such as web design services, social media consulting, and graphic art services are a great fit for teens who want to explore the possibilities of running their own business in the new digital economy. DJ services, rock bands, and even pet sitting services can greatly expand their outreach by posting a digital portfolio that includes photos, video files, and articles that show the world what they can do.

Freelance businesses can give you a way to earn money in your spare time without having to commit to a regular work schedule. In addition to earning money, running an online business while you are still in school can be a great way to gain valuable experience that can help you in the future.

So if you have skills you would like to offer as an online business, you might want to build a digital portfolio to showcase your talent in that area.

Sharing your best work online and encouraging people to view it can open up freelance business opportunities.

would show samples of their work, as well as information on the photographer.

From looking at the photographers' digital portfolios, you could learn about the kinds of photography they specialize in and see if it would meet your needs. This information would help you narrow down the choices of who you might want to hire without having to run all over town and make appointments to look at samples of several photographer's work in person or call or text photographers who might not have the special skills you need. For example, if a photographer's specialty is wedding photos, family portraits, and small children, he or she might not be the best choice if your band needs some exciting performance photos for your website and album cover.

CHAPTER TWO

WHY CREATE A DIGITAL PORTFOLIO?

With so many social networking websites on the internet, such as Facebook, Instagram, and Tumblr where you can express yourself and post about things that interest you, why would you want to go to all the trouble of setting up a digital portfolio to showcase your interests and achievements? Doesn't it take a lot of time to figure out what hosting service to use and learn how to upload all those pictures, blogs, and videos that you might already have up in other places? Don't you need to acquire computer skills you might not already have to set up and build a digital portfolio?

DIGITAL PORTFOLIOS LET THE WORLD KNOW WHAT YOU CAN DO

Actually, there are many good reasons for setting up a digital portfolio to showcase your interests and achievements, and it is a good use of your time and talent. For one thing, having a digital

WHY CREATE A DIGITAL PORTFOLIO? | 17

By creating a digital portfolio, you are letting the world know that you are serious about your interests.

portfolio lets people know that you are serious about putting yourself and your accomplishments out into the world. While posting on Facebook, Instagram, and other social networking websites is a great way of letting your friends know what you are up to, it doesn't necessarily help you connect with people you might want to impress outside of your own social circles. Having a digital portfolio won't automatically put you on the radar of schools, employers, and others you might want to impress, as there are so many digital portfolios on the internet, but it will give you a platform to direct them to.

On top of all the practical reasons for having a digital portfolio to showcase your interests and achievements, many students discover that keeping a digital portfolio gives them a sense of personal ownership of their accomplishments. Posting a digital

YOUR INTERESTS ARE VALUABLE!

Having a digital portfolio that showcases your interests and achievements gives you the opportunity to present the more practical side of interests, which others might tend to view as merely a pastime.

For example, suppose you are deeply interested in graphic novels, superheroes, steampunk literature, and cosplay. Some people might think those kinds of interests have no real-world application, as far as making a living goes. But when doing a research project for school, you discover that this type of literature and the fandom that surrounds it is rapidly growing in popularity, and many businesses have been created to serve the growing fandom. This means that more people will be able to earn an income not only writing, illustrating, and selling these kinds of books, but people are also making a living by designing and selling cosplay costumes for people who enjoy playing characters and by running comic conventions that attract larger numbers of fans every year.

Then, you explain your findings in a well-researched report, blog, or video, and post it on your digital portfolio. Now, your digital portfolio not only showcases your interest in the topic, but it might help convince your parents and teachers that reading, writing, and creating these imaginary works or making cosplay costumes is not a waste of time after all, but can be a valid career path!

The internet and social media apps give people many ways to search, view, and share articles, videos, photos, and other digital content.

portfolio online gives you control over how others see what you are interested in, why you are interested in it, and how you have worked toward accomplishing your goals.

The process of creating a digital portfolio will actually make you the autobiographer of your own interests and learning story! While report cards and parent–teacher conferences tell one side of your learning experience, creating a digital portfolio that showcases your interests and achievements gives you the opportunity to show and explain what you've learned from your own point of view. It also allows you to reach out to others who have similar interests via the internet and exchange ideas and inspire others by showing them what you have accomplished.

WHAT INTERESTS AND ACHIEVEMENTS CAN YOU SHOWCASE?

Digital portfolios can be used to showcase many kinds of accomplishments. In addition to art and photography, which people often think of when they hear the word "portfolio," you can use digital portfolios to showcase projects such as science fair experiments, language arts projects, musical compositions and performances, and sports achievements.

Digital portfolios can be used not only to showcase the best of your school projects, but also interests and achievements you've achieved on your own. Something you learn about while doing an assignment for school can often turn into a new interest that you were not even aware of before.

For example, if you enjoy participating in a makerspace in your school or community, creating a digital portfolio would be a great way to post about your experiences, experiments, and projects. The notes, photographs, and videos you post about your work would not only show anyone who views your digital portfolio what you are capable of, but the information you share could be helpful to other students who are experimenting with similar projects.

ENDLESS USES FOR DIGITAL PORTFOLIOS

Digital portfolios can have many uses, both in and out of school. Some digital portfolio systems, such as Google Sites, Three Ring, Pathbrite, and Evernote have features that allow teachers and other students to view and comment on your work. They can also be used as a place for groups to collaborate on projects where the input of two or more people is needed. That way, you can work online together when that is more practical than meeting in person.

HOW MUCH DOES IT COST?

Many digital platforms are free or have inexpensive plans for students and other users who do not require the more elaborate features found in higher-priced packages. For example, some digital platforms are free unless you require large amounts of data storage, are expecting to have a large number of visitors to your portfolio that might tie up computer servers, or need extra features such as credit card and PayPal acceptance for running an online business.

LET'S GET STARTED!

OK, so you've decided you want to set up a digital portfolio to showcase your interests and achievements, but you need some help deciding where to start. First of all, decide what interests and achievements you want to focus on, and then start thinking about the kind of material you want to post.

GET ALL YOUR FILES TOGETHER

Once you've decided what interests and achievements you want to feature in your portfolio, the next step is to start collecting materials. If you have everything you want to upload in one place, it will make your job a lot easier. It's a good idea to create a folder on your computer where you can store this material, as well as backing it up on a free internet storage service such as OneDrive, Google Cloud Storage, or Dropbox in case something happens to your computer. You might want to have one folder for articles or blog posts, one for photographs, one for art, and one for videos or any other type of file you want to include in your digital portfolio.

If you are including artwork, charts, graphs, or any other visual representation of your work that was not created with a computer program, you will need to photograph it or digitize it with a scanner so you can post it. Many printers used at home or school include scanners and can usually allow you to get a reasonably good representation of your work. If you are taking photographs of your work with a digital camera, make sure the lighting is as good as possible and nothing is making a shadow over the piece you want to photograph.

When you create these folders and files, make sure to give them names that you can immediately recognize. This will make it much easier to find exactly what you need for your digital portfolio without having to do unnecessary searching.

Sometimes materials used in digital portfolios are called artifacts. Artifacts are basically evidence of what you have accomplished. For a digital portfolio about your interests and

WHY CREATE A DIGITAL PORTFOLIO? | 23

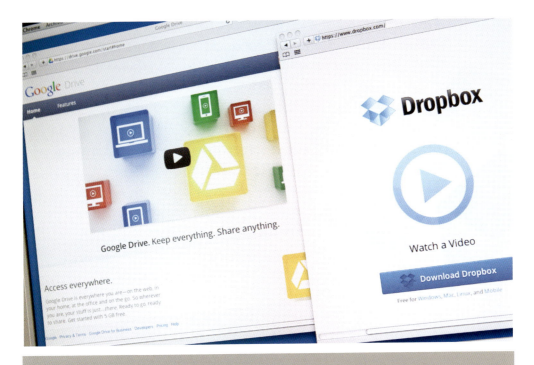

Google Drive and Dropbox are two popular websites for storing and sharing files.

achievements, these artifacts can be writing, photographs, art, video, or other things you created as part of a school project; things you accomplished as extracurricular activities; things you did outside of school; or a combination of all three.

WHAT GOT YOU INTERESTED IN THE FIRST PLACE?

OK, so why is all this so important to you? Have you always been into science, computer coding, sports, art, or drama or is it just something you decided to try last year, then found out you really enjoyed? Is it just a fun activity, or do you have career goals in that field? Those are the kinds of questions viewers of your digital portfolio might have, so it's a good idea to answer them somewhere in your content.

If you are just starting the process of setting up a digital portfolio, you might want to write some blogs about how you first became interested in the achievements you are showcasing and how your interests developed up to this point. Did a teacher, school project, classmate, family member, field trip, book, TV show, or movie first spark your interest? Who or what encouraged you along the way? You might also want to include some early examples of your accomplishments, such as school projects, photographs, drawings, or videos.

Going through the digital portfolio you've used for your school work or paper copies of past assignments and projects can give you some ideas as to things you want to include in a digital portfolio that showcases your interests and achievements.

As your interests and achievements continue to grow through the years, you can someday look back through the posts in your digital portfolio and read the story of how your interests grew and maybe even see some things you've forgotten about.

Besides giving you a way to present your interests to the world over the internet, some high schools now require students to keep digital portfolios as part of their graduation requirement. These portfolios often include assigned projects, but often include work you've done with independent special interest projects as well. These portfolios can help guide students and teachers to a better understanding of how the interests they develop during middle school and high school can best influence their learning path into college and beyond.

WHY CREATE A DIGITAL PORTFOLIO? | 25

Including the story of how you first became interested in an activity and why it is important to you can add a personal touch to your digital portfolio.

Sounds exciting? It certainly can be! While creating a digital portfolio can require that you learn some new skills, such as how to navigate user templates on blogging sites, develop new skills in digital photography and editing, and so on, it doesn't have to be overly complicated. You can start out simple and gain more experience as you go. The process of creating and updating a digital portfolio throughout your school years can help you learn computer skills that will come in handy, regardless of your profession.

CHAPTER THREE

SKILLS FOR CREATING AN OUTSTANDING DIGITAL PORTFOLIO

Sometimes, trying to decide exactly what you want to post and how you want to set up your digital portfolio can feel overwhelming. There is so much to think about when it comes to deciding how to best present your work to the world. And then there are the technical skills of editing photos and videos. But try to relax and take things one step at a time. Everyone who now has a digital portfolio online has gone through the same process. They have succeeded at creating a digital portfolio, and you will too!

With today's user-friendly digital platforms, it is relatively

Today's modern technology makes it easy and affordable to record video presentations about your interests and achievements.

easy to create a basic digital portfolio to showcase your interests and achievements. Many internet digital platforms allow you to create digital portfolios that can include many kinds of digitized media, including blogs and articles, photographs, artwork, videos, audio files, slide shows, charts, and graphs.

But for your portfolio to stand out and get your work noticed, you will want to learn everything you can about making all areas of your presentation look as professional as possible.

LIGHTS, CAMERA, ACTION!

Photographs and videos can add a lot to your digital portfolio. Even if the achievements and interests you want to showcase have nothing to do with becoming a professional photographer, adding photographs and videos to your portfolio can be a very effective way to present your work. Including great photographs and videos will help your portfolio stand out from portfolios or blogs that are nearly all text.

Even if you only know how to take photos and videos on your smartphone, you have the basics down. You have the "raw material," and now you just need to learn a little more about digital editing to make it look even better. This can mean taking classes, reading books, or watching videos about how to take the best digital photos and how to record and edit videos with whatever equipment is available to you.

Many computers, tablets, and smartphones come with software or apps you can use to improve the quality of digital photos and videos. If your device does not have the programs you need, you can download inexpensive, easy-to-use programs.

If you have a Windows computer, you can use free photo editing programs such as Windows Movie Maker, VideoPad Video Editor, and Lightworks. These programs can help you take the material you recorded on a video camera, iPad, or even on a smartphone and make it look more professional. Mac computer users have access to iMovie and other free or inexpensive programs that can do basic video editing and add music, text, and special effects.

Many video editing software programs now have drag-and-drop features that allow you to select and edit video clips, add titles, insert special effects, and add musical soundtracks to your presentation.

In addition to editing programs and apps you can download to your computer, websites such as PicMonkey and Canva allow

Learning about video editing can open doors to a career in video production.

you to edit photos, add text, and experiment with special effects online. Some of these websites, including PicMonkey and Canva, have a basic free version as well as premium features.

If you have access to more expensive photo editing software, such as Photoshop, you will have even more options for making your images look their best. With more advanced programs, such as Photoshop, there is a longer learning curve before you will understand how to use all the features to your best advantage. However, if you do take the time to master the Photoshop software, you will gain a valuable skill many people are willing to pay for.

If your school or community has classes or clubs for people who are interested in digital photography and photo and video editing, try and get involved with them. It can be fun to learn and work in groups where you can help each other and exchange ideas on how to make your digital photography and videos shine.

HYPERLINKS HELP YOU CONNECT

The majority of websites used for digital portfolios allow you to include links from YouTube, Pinterest, Soundcloud, Instagram, Flickr, and other websites where you can upload photographs, videos, blogs, audio recordings, and other material. These links are known as hyperlinks. Hyperlinking allows you to display files that are stored on websites such as YouTube, Pinterest, and Flickr on another website, such as the website you are using for your digital portfolio. Hyperlinks are part of the larger hypertext system that is used throughout the internet to allow internet users to click on a link, text, or picture in one document and be directed to material on an entirely different website. Hypertext is also a way of embedding your email address on a web page so someone can start writing an email to you simply by clicking

YOUTUBE GIVES EVERYONE A CHANCE TO BE A STAR

One of the most exciting things about the internet age has been the democratization of information and entertainment. Anyone who has access to a computer and an email account can post blogs, photos, and videos. When it comes to video sharing, YouTube has been one of the major players. YouTube was founded in 2005 by Chad Hurley, Steve Chen, and Jawed Kairm. They met at college while studying computer science. Within its first year of operation, over 65,000 videos had been uploaded to YouTube and over 100 million viewers per day were going to YouTube to watch videos. The number of YouTube posters and viewers grew even larger as the price of high-speed internet service dropped. Today, more than one billion people a year are watching videos on YouTube.

With such a large viewing audience, posting videos on YouTube with a link to your digital portfolio is likely to increase the number of people who visit it.

Many artists, photographers, singers, songwriters, music groups, fashion designers, makeup artists, video gamers, comedians, political and social commenters, and others have found success by posting videos on YouTube.

If you want to find success on YouTube, it is important not to just post one video, but to keep

(continued on the next page)

HOW TO CREATE DIGITAL PORTFOLIOS TO SHOWCASE YOUR ACHIEVEMENTS AND INTERESTS

(continued from the previous page)

Bethany Morta has gained international fame by video blogging about her interests on YouTube.

posting videos on a regular basis so people who like one video you make will want to come back and view others. This is how you create a YouTube channel, which people can subscribe so they will be notified when you post new videos they might like to see. In addition to having a platform to share their interests, many people who have YouTube channels make money by allowing YouTube video ads before their own videos start.

Bethany Mota is one teenager who made her mark on the world by creating a YouTube video channel that focuses on her interests—makeup, fashion, food, and do-it-yourself decorating projects. She started her video channel in 2009 as a way of expressing herself. Today, her YouTube channel has over 10 million subscribers. Because of her fame on YouTube, Bethany was invited to be a contestant on *Dancing With the Stars*. She was also given the opportunity to interview President Obama and asked him about important issues such as education, jobs, and bullying. This opened up the opportunity for her to be featured in *Teen Vogue*, on National Public Radio, in *People Magazine*, and many other media outlets—which led to even more people subscribing to her YouTube channel. She is now well known as one of the top teenage video bloggers in the United States.

on a link. If you have a Facebook page about your interests and achievements that you want to add a link to on your digital portfolio, you can do that with hypertext as well. There are many tutorials on the internet where you can learn more about hypertext and how it can be used in website design.

ADDING AUDIO FILES TO YOUR PORTFOLIO

With today's technology, it can be easy to record audio files of speeches, presentations, music, or even nature sounds and include them in your digital portfolio. Most computer devices and smartphones allow you to record and store audio files. If you need better sound quality than you can record with your smartphone, iPad, or computer, you might want to think about using a recording studio that has professional microphones as well as soundproofing to keep unwanted sounds, such as traffic noise, from getting into your audio. Perhaps your school or a local organization has a sound studio you can use for free or at a low cost. Once you record the audio file, you can edit it with free audio editing programs such as Audacity. When you are satisfied with the quality of your audio file, you can post it to free websites like Soundcloud, where you can obtain a link to add it to your digital portfolio.

WRITE ALL ABOUT IT!

Whatever interests or achievements you've decided to showcase, it is important to include your best writing samples in a portfolio. Writing about things you have done can play a vital role in presenting your work to the public.

Writing about your interests not only showcases your writing skills, but helps others to see your passion for the things that

SKILLS FOR CREATING AN OUTSTANDING DIGITAL PORTFOLIO | 35

Always remember to proofread your work before posting it online.

interest you. When you write about your interests, think about readers who might be new to the subject of your interest. What would you want to know, for example, if a new friend knew nothing about field hockey, but you wanted to share your love for the game? Try and bring that spark into your writing so that even a person who never thought about that activity might want to know more.

Always remember to spell-check posts before making them public. If the digital platform you are using does not have a spell-checker, you can write your articles or blogs on a word processing program such as Microsoft Word first, then after they have been spell-checked, copy and paste them onto your digital portfolio.

CHAPTER FOUR

WHAT TO INCLUDE IN YOUR DIGITAL PORTFOLIO

So what should you include in your digital portfolio? This can sometimes be a difficult question to answer, especially if you have many interests or have been involved with the activity you want to showcase for a long time and have more artifacts than you need to make a good impression.

Some students choose to create several digital portfolios. You can have one digital portfolio to showcase your academic achievements and other digital portfolios for your personal interests, such as your art or a music group you belong to and would like to promote. If you think that some of the interests you want to create a digital profile about might conflict with your goal of obtaining a job at a certain company or being accepted by a certain college or university, you will want to separate the two. If you want, you can also use different email addresses so you will have a separate identity for each digital portfolio.

Every item you include in your digital portfolio should in some way demonstrate your accomplishments, training, talent, or experience. If you have been engaged in an interest or activity

WHAT TO INCLUDE IN YOUR DIGITAL PORTFOLIO | 37

Posting your achievements on your digital portfolio lets the world know what you can do.

for some time, your more recent works are probably your best. But you may want to include earlier works to show viewers how far you have progressed and how much you learned since you first started. Just make sure to label them so viewers will know why they are being included.

It's a good idea to include a post with each artifact to explain why you chose to include it in your portfolio, as well as any thoughts and feelings, or reflections, about it.

You can also create a digital portfolio to showcase research you have done on an issue that is important to you. Anything that you bring to the public eye could potentially help others. Maybe your research was on the rapid decline of pangolins who are

If you are interested in the quality of food provided by your school lunch program, you can create a digital portfolio to educate the public about your findings.

WHAT TO INCLUDE IN YOUR DIGITAL PORTFOLIO | 39

currently being poached for food and supposed medicine. Your digital portfolio could help teach those who have never heard of this ant-eating creature.

Another example of a digital portfolio was created by the civics students at Roosevelt High School in Chicago, Illinois. They decided to create a digital portfolio to showcase research they had done about the lunch program. They wanted the school to go back to serving lunches cooked at the school instead of buying pre-packaged meals from a company that also provided food to the local prison. They wrote blogs about the lunch program and took photos of the foods they were being served. They made arguments about how much better it would be for students if the schools served healthier foods. They recorded an interview with a teacher who worked at the school when lunches were healthier and made from scratch. And they came up with proposals as to how

YOUR DIGITAL FOOTPRINT

Not all footprints are left by shoes. If you have been on the internet for long, especially on websites such as Facebook, Instagram, and Twitter, you have left a digital footprint that others can view. With search engines such as Google that can quickly scan the internet, anyone thinking about hiring you or admitting you into a college or university can look you up and see posts you made from the beginning of your internet use.

If you have posted comments or photographs that would not make you look good to people you want to impress, the best thing to do is delete them as quickly as possible, and refrain from posting anything that would give a bad impression in the future.

If you want to have social media accounts where you can joke around with your friends and post things you might not necessarily want a future employer or college administrator to see, set up a different account that does not show the public your real name, and have a different account under your real name to build your career and do professional networking.

the school could solve the problem. Those who saw the digital portfolio showcasing the students' concerns wrote comments and encouraged the students to keep asking the school system to provide them with healthier lunches.

WHAT TO INCLUDE IN YOUR DIGITAL PORTFOLIO | 41

IT'S ALL ABOUT YOU!

Since one of the main reasons for creating a digital portfolio is to let people know what you have accomplished, they will need a way to contact you. The best way to do this is by using your email address. Most people have more than one email address: one for friends and family and one for all other uses so that important emails aren't lost in a sea of spam, or emails you don't really want to read. If you are thinking of using your digital profile as a way of going into business, you might want to start a different email address that you'll use only for that purpose.

The digital world offers many ways for people to connect with one another.

INTERNET SAFETY

When you set up a digital portfolio, it's important to keep internet safety in mind. For example, as a student, it's best not to include your street address or phone number. If an employer, college administrator, or group you want to volunteer for needs your phone number, you can give it to them later. Also, make sure to use a secure password that's difficult for anyone to hack.

If anyone is using the email address you use for your digital portfolio to send messages to intimidate or bully you, share

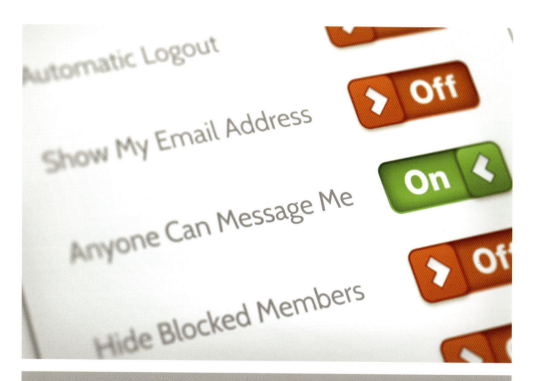

Most social media and digital portfolio websites have settings that let you control who can see your information, as well as how they can contact you.

inappropriate photos or messages, or if you suspect that someone online is not who he or she claims to be, tell your parents and teachers so they can take action to deal with the situation. Also, never agree to meet someone you met online in person unless a parent or other responsible adult is present.

Staysafeonline.org, the website of the National Cyber Security Alliance, is a good resource for information on online safety issues.

CHAPTER FIVE

WHAT DIGITAL PLATFORM SHOULD I USE?

There are many platforms you can use to host a digital portfolio. A digital platform is the computer hardware and software that hosts websites or internet services. The entry page for most digital platforms is a signup page where new users can open accounts and current users can log in to work on their blog or portfolio.

Some digital platforms are large and known by nearly everyone, but others are relatively small, such as a computer server owned by a small local company. On the larger end of the spectrum, Facebook is a digital platform. So are Google, Twitter, Instagram, Wordpress, YouTube, and LinkedIn.

There are many platforms available that can host your digital portfolio.

CODING YOUR OWN DIGITAL PORTFOLIO

If you have coding skills and want other people to know about it, why not write the code on your own digital portfolio? While the digital platforms many people use for their portfolios work fine without any knowledge of code, others can be modified. Wordpress is one popular blog site that allows users to write their own HTML code to modify the appearance of blogs and portfolios. It can be used with the visual editor to post without coding, or you can switch to the HTML text editor and write your own code. If you are interested in learning more about HTML coding, there are many excellent books available about coding and website design, as well as tutorials, on the internet.

Knowing how to write HTML code and design websites is a valuable skill, as some businesses and organizations prefer personally designed websites to those with options limited to filling in spaces in website templates.

If you decide to write your own code for your digital portfolio, it's a good idea to check and see how the finished portfolio looks on various devices, such as standard computers, smartphones, tablets, and iPads.

Some digital platforms allow users to write their own HTML code.

Even if your teachers have a platform they want you to use for a digital portfolio that contains your classwork, you have the option of creating your own digital portfolio to showcase your interests and achievements that you can use outside of school. In fact, you might decide to create a separate digital portfolio for all your interests! Some options you might want to consider are Google Sites, Behance, Wordpress, Blogger, Flickr, Weebly, and Wix.

Setting up a digital portfolio can be an exciting project. There are so many decisions to be made as to the digital platform, background color or patterns, type of font you can use, and choice of photos and videos. The features offered on the free versions of these platforms change, so the best way to learn about them is to go online and check them out.

CAN THE PLATFORM HOLD ALL YOUR STUFF?

Before you start a digital portfolio, it's a good idea to check and make sure the platform you are using can support the kind of material you want to use. Is it easy to upload photos and make them appear the size you want? Is it easy to move elements around on the page? Do you have a choice about the order your blog posts appear in, or will they appear in the order they were posted? Is there a way to have an "About Me" section or some other intro page that can always be seen when someone looks at your digital portfolio? Do you have the option to have multiple pages or sections on your digital portfolio that people can scan while on the introductory page?

Is the limit on how much data you can upload sufficient for your needs? If not, is it relatively easy to add links to other websites such as YouTube or Flickr and make the videos or images show up on your page the size and position you want them?

WHAT DIGITAL PLATFORM SHOULD I USE? | 47

Some platforms allow you to see how your blog or digital portfolio will appear on various devices.

Those are all things you will probably want to consider when choosing a digital platform for your work. Sometimes experimenting with various platform sites is the best way to see if they meet your needs. You might want to sign up with several free digital platforms and experiment with their website's features before making your final decision.

If you know how to write code, you might look for a platform that allows you to use your coding skills to personalize your digital portfolio to a greater degree. If coding skills are something you would like to showcase, this should be an especially important consideration.

If you enjoy designing websites from scratch and would like to showcase that skill, your choices for a digital platform would be different from someone who wants an easy-to-use, less complicated way of presenting his or her work.

CHAPTER SIX

BEYOND CREATING A DIGITAL PORTFOLIO

Once you have created a digital portfolio, how you use it is up to you. You can post links to your digital portfolio on websites where you want to introduce yourself and your work.

If you are looking for a job, you can include your résumé on your portfolio and have it ready to send to potential employers.

LinkedIn Higher Education is a valuable resource for students to find jobs and connect with colleges and universities.

GETTING LINKED INTO LINKEDIN

The career building networking website LinkedIn was once only for adults, but now anyone thirteen and older can create a profile. LinkedIn Higher Education gives students an

49

opportunity to post a profile with a résumé that can help them find jobs or get into college. LinkedIn Higher Education's website has useful articles on how to build a great student profile, tailoring your profile to your goals, building your personal brand, and how to network and search for jobs or internships.

Business-oriented social networking websites such as LinkedIn can help you connect with people who are responsible for hiring in your field, as well as receive recommendations from people who have seen your accomplishments.

KEEPING THINGS PROFESSIONAL

If the digital portfolio you are creating is mostly intended to impress employers or school administrators, make sure to include a professional looking photo of yourself, as well as information about your education, jobs you've had and volunteer experiences, samples of your work, and anything else that would be likely to interest them.

Many job search websites such as Indeed allow job seekers to post links to digital portfolios as part of their applications, giving employers a better understanding of their accomplishments than merely listing things they've done on a job application.

SHOWCASE YOUR SKILLS ON BEHANCE

Behance is a relatively new digital platform many people are using to post portfolios that showcase their talents. Many graphic artists, web designers, and other creative professionals use it to gain visibility for their work and find clients. In addition to serving the professional arts community, Behance has a special area of their website dedicated to student portfolios and projects where they

BEYOND CREATING A DIGITAL PORTFOLIO | 51

Digital platforms such as Behance provide opportunities for you to have your work seen by the right people.

can gain recognition for their work. Behance hosts competitions for students, including the Adobe Design Achievement Awards and the AWARD School Portfolio where they recognize the portfolios of students that show exceptional talent.

TEEN'S DIGITAL PORTFOLIO LEADS TO FASHION PHOTOGRAPHY FAME

Ann He, who is now known as an international fashion photographer, got her start when she was fifteen years old and living in Dallas, Texas. She loved taking pictures and found that collaborating with friends who were aspiring models and makeup artists in need of quality photographs was a perfect way to develop her skills and create her own unique photographic style, which incorporates elements of nature and mystery into traditional fashion photography.

Ann posted the unique fashion photographs she took of her friends to her digital portfolio on Flickr, not knowing who might view them. Soon, her photographs were being featured on Flickr's Explore tab, which helped her work gain even more exposure. This resulted in Ann's work being published in international fashion magazines and on blogs and websites.

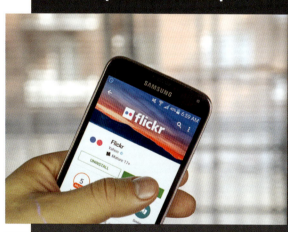

Ann He started her career as a fashion photographer by posting her best photographic work on Flickr.

LET'S COLLABORATE!

You can also use the skills you showcase in your digital portfolio as a way of reaching out to other people you might want to collaborate with. For example, if you are an artist or graphic designer and you want to get into illustrating or creating covers for books, creating a digital portfolio focusing on your accomplishments in those areas can help you connect with authors who need those services. Once you create a digital portfolio that showcases your talents, you can use it to look for work or volunteer opportunities where you can build your skills while helping others.

THE WHOLE WORLD IS WATCHING!

According to the United Nations, there are over 3 billion people on the internet, so you have a good chance of connecting with someone who needs your services and wants to hire or collaborate with you! Sometimes, setting up a digital portfolio and letting people know what you can do can even lead to collaborations within your own school or community.

THE FUTURE OF THE INTERNET

Looking back over the past 20 years or so, the ways people use the internet have continually grown and changed. Businesses have started where the items sold are totally digitized, such as the e-book self-publishing industry. Etsy's website has allowed people to make arts and crafts at home and sell them to a worldwide market. Online classes where the teacher and participants have never met in person help people learn what they need to

Websites such as Etsy allow craftspeople to sell their work to customers all over the world.

achieve their goals. People have posted videos on YouTube just for fun and have become TV stars as a result.

What's next? No one really knows. But having a digital portfolio that showcases your interests and achievements and keeping it updated on a regular basis will help you be ready to meet the challenges of today and give you a head start at being able to take advantage of the opportunities to come in the high-tech world of tomorrow.

GLOSSARY

artifact An item that shows evidence of learning, skills, discovery, or achievement that can be included in a portfolio.
blog Journal entries or articles posted online.
cloud storage A method for storing electronic data or files where information is stored on remote servers and can be accessed through the internet.
coding Writing information needed to design a website using HTML or another programming language.
collaborate Two or more people working together on a project.
digital footprint Information your activities online leave that others can view.
digital platform A web hosting service for websites, blogs, and digital portfolios.
digital portfolio An electronic portfolio that can contain writing, photographs, videos, and other content.
digitize To change information, photographs, art, or sound into a digital form that can be stored and shared through the internet.
drag-and-drop A system used by many video editing programs where the user can rearrange videos, titles, effects, or other content by selecting it and moving it to a different location.
HTML Hypertext markup language is the programming language used to control how web pages are displayed.
hyperlink A link that directs computer users to information at another location.
hypertext Text on a website or computer document that includes a hyperlink.

LinkedIn A business and career networking website.

makerspace An area where people who are interested in experimenting can get together to work on projects and explore new ideas.

scanner A device that converts photos, documents, and art into digital files that can be stored on a computer, uploaded to websites, or emailed to other internet users.

steampunk Science fiction or fantasy stories that take place in an imaginary time where steam power is often used in place of electricity. Steampunk stories often take place in the 1800s.

template A pre-designed website, blog, or digital profile hosting site where users can add content without having to write their own HTML code.

World Wide Web An international system of computer servers that was designed to allow users to view and post content that is viewed through web pages.

FOR MORE INFORMATION

Association for Authentic, Experiential and Evidence-Based Learning
4060 Post Road, Attn: AAEEBL
Warwick, RI 02886 USA
(401) 884-5300
Website: http://www.aaeebl.org
This professional nonprofit has a goal of promoting digital-based portfolio learning as a major way to transform higher education.

Canadian Education Association
60 St. Clair Avenue East, Suite 703
Toronto, ON, M4T 1N5
(866) 803-9549
Website: http://www.cea-ace.ca
This organization is working to improve education throughout Canada, including bringing technology into the learning process.

Connect to Learning
The Making Connections National Resource Center
LaGuardia Community College
31-10 Thomson Ave, Room M405
Long Island City, NY 11101
Website: http://c2l.mcnrc.org
This network of e-portfolio leaders is working to bring digital portfolios into wider use in public and private schools.

Media Smarts
205 Catherine Street, Suite 100
Ottawa, ON K2P 1C3
Canada
Website: http://mediasmarts.ca

This organization develops digital and media literacy programs and resources for homes, schools, and communities throughout Canada.

MERLOT ePortfolio Portal
California State University
1250 N Bellflower Boulevard
Long Beach, CA 90840
Website: http://eportfolio.merlot.org
A program of the California State University, this resource is designed to help students and educators around the world implement digital portfolios in education.

Technology Student Association
1914 Association Drive
Reston, VA 20191-1540
(888) 860-9010
Website: http://www.tsaweb.org
This national organization of students is engaged in science, technology, engineering, and mathematics studies. Its primary supports are teachers, parents, and business leaders who believe in the need for a technologically literate society. One of their goals is to help students design websites and digital portfolios.

WEBSITES

Because of the changing nature of internet links, Rosen Publishing has developed an online list of websites related to the subject of this book. This site is updated regularly. Please use this link to access the list:

http://www.rosenlinks.com/PROJL/showcase

FOR FURTHER READING

Cooper, Nate, and Kim Gee. *Build Your Own Website: A Comic Guide to HTML, CSS, and Wordpress.* San Francisco, CA: No Starch Press, 2014.

Croce, Nicolas. *Enhancing Your Academic Digital Footprint* (Digital and Information Literacy). New York, NY: Rosen Central, 2012.

Culbertson, Melissa. *Blog Design For Dummies.* Hoboken, NJ: For Dummies, 2013.

Davis, Anne P., and Ewa McGrail. *Student Blogs: How Online Writing Can Transform Your Classroom.* Lanham, MD: Rowman & Littlefield, 2016.

Fromm, Megan. *Digital Content Creation* (Media Literacy) New York, NY: Rosen Young Adult, 2015.

Hatter, Clyde. *Coderdojo Nono: Build Your Own Website: Create With Code*: Hampshire, UK: Egmont Books, 2016.

Landau, Jennifer. *Cybercitizenship: Online Rights and Responsibilities* (Helpline: Teen Issues and Answers). New York, NY. Rosen Publishing, 2013.

Martin, Chris. *Build Your Own Website* (Quick Expert's Guide). New York, NY: Rosen Classroom, 2014.

Willett, Edward. *Career Building Through Using Digital Design Tools* (Digital Career Building). New York, NY. Rosen Publishing, 2014.

Young, Jennifer. *Picture Perfect Social Media: A Handbook for Styling Perfect Photos for Posting, Blogging, and Sharing.* London, UK: Apple Press, 2014.

BIBLIOGRAPHY

Carlisle, Jennifer. "3 Ways Digital Portfolios Benefit Your Students." *Art of Education*, 2015. Retrieved November 18, 2016. https://www.theartofed.com/2015/11/04/3-ways-digital-portfolios-benefit-your-students.

Daley, Bill. "Students Boycott Roosevelt's School Lunch." *Chicago Tribune*, December 7, 2015. http://www.chicagotribune.com/dining/ct-student-boycott-school-lunch-chicago-theodore-roosevelt-high-story.html.

Dunham, Erika. "Grades 6–8: Digital Portfolios Close Out the Year with Reflection, Celebration, and Meaningful Projects." *Scholastic*. Retrieved November 18, 2016. http://www.scholastic.com/teachers/article/grades-6-8-digital-portfolios.

Friday, Leslie. "E-Portfolios Showcase Student Work: Another 'Arrow in the Quiver' in Job Hunt." *BU Today*, January 31, 2012. https://www.bu.edu/today/2012/e-portfolios-showcase-student-word.

GTC Team. "How Do Digital Portfolios Help Students?" *Global Digital Citizen*. Retrieved November 18, 2016. https://globaldigitalcitizen.org/how-do-digital-portfolios-help-students.

Hicks, Kristen. "5 Free Tools For Making Digital Portfolios." *Edudemic*, February 9, 2015. http://www.edudemic.com/tools-for-digital-portfolios.

Hiles, Heather. "Digital Portfolios Position Students for Success in the Workforce." *EdSurge News*, July 6, 2016. https://www.edsurge.com/news/2016-07-06-digital-portfolios-position-students-for-success-in-the-workforce.

Kolonia, Peter. "Five Under 20: Young Photographers You Should Know." *Popular Photography*, April 22, 2014. http://www.popphoto.com/photos/2014/04/five-under-20-young-photographers-you-should-know.

Korbey, Holly. "What Will Digital Portfolios Mean for College-Bound Students?" *KQED News*, March 22, 2016. https://ww2.kqed.org/mindshift/2016/03/22/what-will-digital-portfolios-mean-for-college-bound-students.

Penn State. "Effective Technical Writing in the Information Age: Online Portfolios." *Penn State*. Retrieved November 18, 2016. https://www.e-education.psu.edu/styleforstudents/c7_p5.html.

Sivek, Susan Currie. "Journalism Students: Tools for Jazzing Up Your Portfolio." *Mediashift*, March 11, 2014. http://mediashift.org/2014/03/portfolio-options-for-journalism-and-media-students.

Swallow, Erica. "The New High School Essentials: LinkedIn, a Resumé, and a Digital Portfolio." *Huffington Post*, September 11, 2016. http://www.huffingtonpost.com/erica-swallow/the-new-high-school-essen_b_8106544.html.

Teacher Tap. "Electronic Portfolios: Students, Teachers, and Life Long Learners." Retrieved November 18, 2016. http://eduscapes.com/tap/topic82.htm.

Team FindSpark. "Examples of Stellar Student and Recent Grad Creative Online Portfolios." *FindSpark*, January 7, 2016. https://www.findspark.com/creative-online-portfolios-students-recent-grads.

Vander Ark, Tom. "Every Student Should Have a Digital Portfolio." *Getting Smart*, June 26, 2015. http://www.gettingsmart.com/2015/06/every-student-should-have-a-digital-portfolio.

INDEX

A

artifacts, 22–23, 36–36
artist, 4, 7–9, 13, 31, 52, 53
Audacity, 34
audio, 28, 30, 34
author, 4, 53

B

Behance, 12, 46, 50–51
blog, 10–11, 13, 16, 18, 22, 24, 26, 28, 30–33, 35, 39, 44–47, 52
Blogger, 11, 33, 46
Blogspot, 11

C

Canva, 29–30
clients, 4, 50
cloud storage, 22, 30, 34
coding, 6, 10, 11, 23, 45, 48
collaboration, 21, 52, 53
college, 4, 6, 24, 31, 36, 40, 42, 49, 50
context, 23–26
cosplay, 18–19
cost, 6, 21, 34

D

Deviantart, 12
digital camera, 10, 22
digital footprint, 40
digital portfolio
    components, 28–35
    early technology, 10–11
    forms, 11–12
    purpose, 4–10, 16–20
digitizing materials, 22, 28, 53
Dropbox, 22, 23

E

e-book, 53
editing, 6, 26–30, 34
email, 4, 11, 13, 30, 31, 36, 41, 42
employers, 4, 17, 40, 42, 49, 50

F

Facebook, 16, 17, 34, 40, 44
Flickr, 12, 30, 46, 52

G

Google, 13, 21, 22, 23, 40, 44, 46
graduation requirement, 24

H

hosting service, 6, 16
HTML, 10, 45
hyperlinks, 4, 11, 13, 30, 31, 34, 46, 50
hypertext, 10, 30–31, 34

I

Instagram, 16, 17, 30, 40, 44
internet safety, 42–43
item selection, 36–43

62

L

Lightworks, 28
LinkedIn, 44, 49, 50

M

makerspace, 20
Mota, Bethany, 33
Movie Maker, 28

N

National Cyber Security Alliance, 42

O

OneDrive, 22
online businesses, 14, 21
organization, 22–23

P

Pathbrite, 21
PayPal, 21
photographer, 4, 12, 13, 15, 28, 31, 52
photography, 8, 12, 15, 20, 26, 30, 52
photos, 4, 10, 11, 13–15, 19, 27, 28–31, 39, 43, 46
Photoshop, 30
physical portfolio, 8–10
PicMonkey, 29–30
Pinterest, 30
platforms, 44–48

R

résumé, 49, 50

S

smartphone, 28, 29, 34
social networking, 14, 16–17, 19, 31, 40, 42, 50
Soundcloud, 30, 34
spam, 41
spell-check, 35

T

templates, 11, 26, 45
Three Ring, 21
Tumblr, 16

U

United Nations, 53

V

valuable interests, 18–19
Video Editor, 28
videos, 4, 10–11, 13, 16, 19–20, 22, 24, 27–31, 33, 46, 54
VideoPad, 28

W

Weebly, 11, 46
Wix, 11, 46
Wordpress, 11, 44–46
writing samples, 4, 7, 8, 11, 34–35

Y

YouTube, 30–33, 44, 46, 54

ABOUT THE AUTHOR

Anita Louise McCormick has been interested in science, technology, and electronic communication for many years. She is the author of over a dozen nonfiction books, including *Shortwave Radio Listening for Beginners* and *The Shortwave Listener's Q & A Book*, published by TAB/McGraw-Hill; *The Telephone and Telegraph in American History,* Enslow Publishing; and *10 Great Makerspace Projects for Language Arts*, Rosen Publishing.

PHOTO CREDITS

Cover Hill Street Studios/Blend Images/Getty Images; p. 5 © iStockphoto.com/demaerre; pp. 8–9 Fedorova Nataliia/Shutterstock.com; pp. 12–13 © iStockphoto.com/CentrallTAlliance; p. 14 Halfpoint/Shutterstock.com; p. 17 KP Photograph/Shutterstock.com; p. 19 © iStockphoto.com/Rawpixel; p. 23 © iStockphoto.com/Alberto Bogo; p. 25 SG SHOT/Shutterstock.com; p. 27 Hero Images/Getty Images; p. 29 © iStockphoto.com/eldinhoid; p. 32 Rob Kim/FilmMagic, Inc/Getty Images; p. 35 © iStockphoto.com/ogichobanov; p. 37 focal point/Shutterstock.com; pp. 38–39 asiseeit/E+/Getty Images; p. 41 Alexey Boldin/Shutterstock.com; p. 42 SpiffyJ/E+/Getty Images; pp. 44, 47 Rawpixel.com/Shutterstock.com; p. 45 Mclek/Shutterstock.com; p. 49 mirtmirt/Shutterstock.com; p. 51 © iStockphoto.com/Mutlu Kurtbas; p. 52 dennizn/Shutterstock.com; p. 54 haveseen/Shutterstock.com; interior pages graphic pp. 7, 16, 27, 36, 44, 49 Ron Dale/Shutterstock.com.

Design: Michael Moy
Editor and Photo Researcher: Ellina Litmanovich